All Kinds of Rocks

Lorraine Harrison

New York

Published in 2014 by The Rosen Publishing Group, Inc.
29 East 21st Street, New York, NY 10010

Copyright © 2014 by The Rosen Publishing Group, Inc.

All rights reserved. No part of this book may be reproduced in any form without permission in writing from the publisher, except by a reviewer.

Book Design: Katelyn Londino

Photo Credits: Cover Corepics VOF/Shutterstock.com; p. 5 (castle) Pecold/Shutterstock.com; p. 5 (arrowhead) I. Pilon/Shutterstock.com; p. 7 (talc in rock form) ERIC CABANIS/AFP/Getty Images; p. 7 (talc in powder form) GVictoria/Shutterstock.com; p. 9 (dunite) B.navez/Wikipedia.org; pp. 9 (gabbro), 13 Tyler Boyes/Shutterstock.com; p. 11 Martin Fowler/Shutterstock.com; p. 15 (gneiss) LesPalenik/Shutterstock.com; p. 15 (hornfels) Fed/Wikipedia.org; p. 17 (hands holding rock) Dervin Witmer/Shutterstock.com; p. 17 (person standing by boulder) AISPIX by Image Source/Shutterstock.com; p. 17 (climber on mountains) Galyna Andrushko/Shutterstock.com; p. 19 (mountain) Vadim Petrakov/Shutterstock.com; p. 19 (sand) Alexey V Smirnov/Shutterstock.com; p. 21 (turtle fossil) Mike Brake/Shutterstock.com; p. 21 (shells fossil) Michal Ninger/Shutterstock.com; p. 21 (shell prints, dinosaur prints) Dreamframer/Shutterstock.com; p. 22 iStockphoto/Thinkstock.com.

ISBN: 978-1-4777-2407-1
6-pack ISBN: 978-1-4777-2408-8

Manufactured in the United States of America

CPSIA Compliance Information: Batch #CS13RC: For further information contact Rosen Publishing, New York, New York at 1-800-237-9932.

Contents

Using Rocks	4
Hardness	6
Texture	8
Color	12
Size	16
Fossils	20
Different Kinds of Fossils	21
Rocks Are Everywhere!	22
Glossary	23
Index	24

Using Rocks

There are so many rocks in this world! Rocks have different characteristics, or things that make them look and feel special. They're used for different things because of their characteristics. Some people use rocks to build things. Some people use rocks as tools.

> People made this castle and this tool hundreds of years ago. They're both made from rocks.

Hardness

Rocks are hard objects that are made of **minerals**. Some minerals are harder than others. The Mohs scale is used to tell how hard a mineral is. To test a mineral for hardness, you **scratch** it with another mineral. A harder mineral can scratch a softer one.

Talc is the lowest mineral on the Mohs scale. It's very soft and can be scratched by any other mineral.

Texture

The way a rock feels is called its texture. Some rocks feel **rough** when you hold them. These rocks have big **grains**. That's what makes them feel bumpy. Gabbro (GA-broh) is a rock that's rough because it has big grains. Dunite (DOO-nyt) is another rough rock. It has big grains called crystals.

> Gabbro and dunite are both rough rocks. You can see each grain.

Sometimes water and other forces wear down a rock's bumps. This is called weathering. Rocks without bumps are smooth. They're sometimes found in places with a lot of water, like rivers. Some rocks, such as slate, are smooth because they have small grains.

Slate is made of tiny grains of clay. It's smooth to the touch.

Color

Not all rocks are gray! Rocks come in many different colors. Some are pink, like gypsum (JIHP-suhm). Others are green, red, black, or yellow. The colors depend on which minerals are in the rock. Some rocks have more than one color. For example, diorite is gray, black, and white.

Diorite is made of both light and dark minerals.

13

Some rocks have different colors that form a **pattern**. Gneiss (NYS) is a rock that has stripes of different colors. These look like bands that circle the rock. Hornfels (HOHRN-fehlz) is another rock with stripes of different colors. The stripes show that a rock is made of more than one mineral.

Have you ever seen rocks with patterns on them?

Size

Rocks are some of the biggest things in this world. Some rocks, called stones, are as big as a football. Some rocks, called boulders, are as big as people. The biggest rocks that we can see make up mountains. What's the biggest rock you've ever seen?

> Big rocks can be fun to climb! People come from all over the world to climb tall mountains.

Rocks don't always stay the same. A rock will always have the same hardness and color, but its size can change. Sometimes big rocks break down into smaller rocks. Some rocks, called pebbles, are as small as a penny. Sand is one of the smallest kinds of rocks.

It's easy to find sand on a beach because water breaks big rocks down into smaller ones.

Fossils

Rocks can tell a story. For example, some rocks have fossils (FAH-suhlz) in them. Fossils are remains or prints of a plant or animal. They were preserved, or saved, in rocks millions of years ago. Fossils can tell us when and where animals and plants lived and died.

Trace fossils are more common than body fossils.

Different Kinds of Fossils

body fossils:
remains of something that was once living

bones

shells

trace fossils:
signs that something was once present

footprints

shell prints

21

Rocks Are Everywhere!

Each rock is different. Rocks can be big or small, rough or smooth. They come in many different colors. They can be found in the tallest mountains and in the deepest oceans. They can even be found right under our feet! What kinds of rocks have you seen?

Glossary

grain (GRAYN) A tiny, hard piece of something.

mineral (MIH-nuh-ruhl) Something in the earth that is not living.

pattern (PA-tuhrn) Shapes, lines, and colors that appear over and over.

rough (RUHF) Not smooth.

scratch (SKRACH) To cut or tear.

Index

characteristics, 4

color(s), 12, 14, 18, 22

crystals, 8

diorite, 12

dunite, 8

fossils, 20, 21

gabbro, 8

gneiss, 14

grain(s), 8, 10

gypsum, 12

hardness, 6, 18

hornfels, 14

mineral(s), 6, 12, 14

Mohs scale, 6

mountains, 16, 22

pattern(s), 14

size, 16, 18

slate, 10

talc, 6

texture, 8

tool(s), 4

weathering, 10